A Gift

For: Maycee
my darlin' grand-daughter
From: Nonny

I love you
so much. You
are always in my heart.

Little Birthday Wishes

Illustrated by Becky Kelly

Written by Patrick Regan

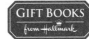

GIFT BOOKS
from Hallmark

Andrews McMeel Publishing

BOK4093

This edition published in 2003 by Andrews McMeel Publishing
exclusively for Hallmark Cards, Inc.
www.hallmark.com

ISBN: 0-7407-3792-9

Illustrations by Becky Kelly
Design by Stephanie Farley
Edited by Jean Lowe
Production by Elizabeth Nuelle

It seems that birthday wishes
have a way of coming true
so I'm sending up some little wishes
to rain
down
on you.

I wish you clear eyes
and an open heart

to better take in
all the beauty that surrounds you.

I wish you a soul that is light,
a spirit that soars,

and a mind alive with
private dreams and powerful ideas.

I wish you the companionship
of those you love most,

And the pleasure
of your own company
in those times
you'd rather be alone.

I wish for you golden memories
of cherished moments,

B. Kelly

whose luster only increases
with the passing of time;

And I hope that memories
of this birthday
will fit snugly into
your box of treasured recollections.

I wish for you
fresh-picked berries,
warm soothing tea,
and your favorite dessert
(for breakfast if you like!)

I wish you carefree giggles with friends,
familiar hands to hold,
and a sense of belonging
no matter where you are.

I wish for you pleasant surprises,

Both slight and grand,

And the never-ending ability
to find true joy in life's little gifts.

And as you grow older,
I wish for you the continued ability
to focus on the growing
rather than the older.

I wish for you the peace
that comes from believing in yourself

and the joy to be found
in doing for others.

B. Kelly

And I truly hope you realize
the love that so many feel for you.

And as all these wishes fall softly
around your feet,

I'll add just one more wish:

That all of your
fondest birthday wishes
will come true.

Becky Kelly captures in her watercolor illustrations the magic of her youth in West Virginia. As a popular greeting card artist, Becky's sentiments have won a devoted following throughout the country. She lives in Kansas City, Missouri, with her nine-year-old son Payton (who took the above photo of his mom).

Andrews McMeel
Publishing
an Andrews McMeel Universal company

www.beckykelly.com